HOT &
SPICY

Consultant Editor:
Valerie Ferguson

HERMES
HOUSE

Contents

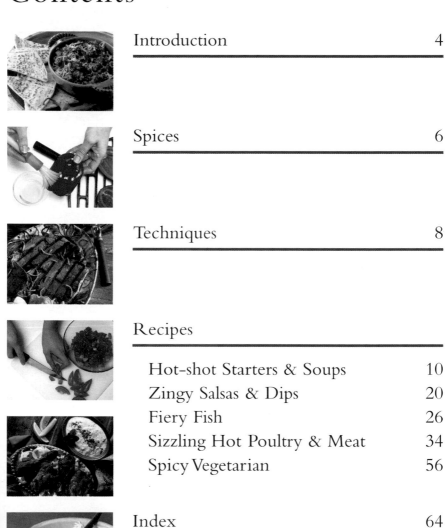

Introduction

If variety is the spice of life, it certainly must be said that spices give life – or at least food – its variety.

In all their idiosyncratic guises, spices lend richness, heat and complexity to literally every food imaginable, and it is impossible to conceive of a cuisine that does not benefit from unique and distinctive spicing. In fact, from the sun-drenched Caribbean to the bustling sidewalk-stalls of Thailand and the spirited southwestern United States, "hot and spicy" defines good eating for millions of people who would not dream of consuming bland, unseasoned food when piquant delights are available at every turn.

Spices are nothing if not highly individual, well-defined and capable of transforming dishes with a single pinch. Indeed, for thousands of years, the right spice, or combination of spices, has helped define a nation's or a people's cuisine. Spices, once a valuable and precious commodity, are now readily available. Using them makes dining an adventure. Within the pages of *Hot & Spicy* you will find an exhilarating, mind-expanding and palate-tingling collection of recipes from every corner of the world, from the fiery heat of Thailand's Hot-and-sour Prawn Soup, to the eye-watering North African Vegetable Couscous with Saffron & Harissa. Dishes to savour and to set your taste buds alight.

Spices

It is the blending of spices and flavourings that gives food its character.

CHILLIES AND CAYENNE
Fresh and dried chillies add heat, and vary according to size and colour. Generally, but not always, large, pale green chillies will be milder than small, red ones. Dried chillies are always hotter than fresh. Cayenne is a very hot chilli. Always wash your hands thoroughly after preparing chillies and if possible wear thin rubber gloves.

CORIANDER
One of the most popular spices, these small, beige seeds are used whole and ground, giving a slightly sweet flavour. Fresh coriander leaves are used for flavouring and as a garnish.

CUMIN
"White" cumin seeds are oval, ridged and greenish brown in colour. They have a strong aroma and flavour and can be used whole or ground. Ready-ground cumin powder is widely available. Black cumin seeds are dark and aromatic and are used to flavour curries and rice. They can be found in Asian stores.

CURRY POWDER
There are many variations of this spice mixture, varying in both flavour and colour. Traditionally, Indian curry powder is a combination of freshly ground turmeric, cumin and coriander seeds.

FIVE-SPICE POWDER
This reddish-brown powder, used extensively in Chinese cooking, is a combination of five ground spices – star anise, fennel, cloves, cinnamon and Sichuan pepper. Used sparingly, it has a wonderful flavour, but it can be dominant if too much is added.

GARAM MASALA
This is a mixture of spices which can be made from freshly ground spices at home or purchased ready-made. There is no set recipe, but a typical mixture might include black cumin seeds, peppercorns, cloves, cinnamon and black cardamom pods.

GARLIC
Available fresh and dried, garlic is used for its strong flavour.

GINGER, FRESH
Fresh root ginger is the plump, bulbous rhizome of the ginger plant. It is knobbly and should be peeled thinly with a potato peeler or sharp knife and chopped or grated. It has a hot, sharp, fresh taste quite different from ground ginger which is hot and peppery.

HARISSA
A fiery-hot paste used mostly in North African cookery. It is made from a blend of chillies, garlic, cumin, coriander and cayenne and can be bought in small jars.

MUSTARD
Comes as brown, black or white seed as well as traditional mustard powder (ground mustard seed blended with turmeric). Used sparingly it is a great flavour enhancer for many cheese and egg sauces.

PAPRIKA
A sweet, piquant spice, ideal for enhancing the flavour of vegetables, poultry and meat. Spanish paprika is milder than the Hungarian variety.

PEPPERCORNS
Pepper is a universal seasoning. Dried black and white peppercorns are best freshly ground for maximum pungency. Green peppercorns are available fresh, bottled in brine or dried. Sichuan and pink peppercorns are also now available.

TURMERIC
Like saffron, turmeric gives a rich yellow colour to any sauce. Use in moderation, as too much will leave an acrid, bitter taste.

Techniques

CRUSHING SPICES

Some spices are used whole, but where they are crushed or ground, the best flavour will be obtained if you start off with whole spices and crush them as and when needed.

1 Crush whole spices in a coffee grinder or spice mill.

2 Alternatively, use a pestle and mortar, especially for small quantities of spices.

PREPARING FRESH GINGER

Fresh root ginger can be used in slices, strips or finely chopped.

1 Peel the tough skin off the root with a peeler or a small, sharp knife. Then cut into thin strips, using a large, sharp knife.

2 Place each piece flat on a chopping board, cut into fine strips and use, or turn the strips around and chop them finely.

PREPARING CHILLIES

Chillies add a distinct flavour. The seeds can be left in for a hotter result.

1 Always protect your hands, as chillies can irritate the skin; wear rubber gloves and never rub your eyes after handling chillies. Halve the chilli lengthways and remove and discard the seeds.

2 Slice, finely chop and use as required. Wash the knife and board thoroughly in hot, soapy water. Always wash your hands scrupulously after preparing chillies.

PREPARING GARLIC

Don't worry if you don't have a garlic press: try this method, which gives wonderful, juicy results.

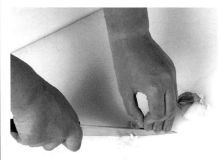

1 Break the clove of garlic off the bulb. Place the flat side of a large knife on top and strike with your fist. Remove all the papery outer skin. Begin by finely chopping the clove.

2 Sprinkle over a little table salt and, using the flat side of a large knife blade, work the salt into the garlic, until the clove softens and releases its juices. Use as required.

Guacamole

Nachos or tortilla chips are the perfect accompaniment for this dip.

Serves 4

INGREDIENTS
2 ripe avocados
2 red chillies, seeded
1 garlic clove
1 shallot
30 ml/2 tbsp olive oil, plus extra to serve
juice of 1 lemon
salt
flat leaf parsley leaves, to garnish

1 Halve the avocados, remove the stones and, using a spoon, scoop out the flesh into a bowl.

2 Mash the flesh well with a potato masher or a large fork.

3 Finely chop the chillies, garlic and shallot, then stir into the mashed avocado with the olive oil and lemon juice. Add salt to taste.

4 Spoon the mixture into a small serving bowl. Drizzle over a little olive oil and scatter with a few flat leaf parsley leaves. Serve immediately.

VARIATION: You can make a completely smooth guacamole by whizzing the ingredients in a blender or food processor. If you prefer a chunkier version, add a diced tomato or red pepper.

Garlic Prawns with Chillies

For this simple Spanish tapas dish you really need fresh raw prawns.

Serves 4

INGREDIENTS
350–450 g/12 oz–1 lb large raw prawns
2 red chillies
75 ml/5 tbsp extra virgin olive oil
3 garlic cloves, crushed
salt and freshly ground black pepper

1 Remove the heads and shells from the prawns, leaving the tails intact.

2 Halve each chilli lengthways and discard the seeds. Heat the oil in a flameproof pan suitable for serving. (Alternatively use a frying pan and have a warmed serving dish ready in the oven.)

3 Add all the prawns, chilli and garlic to the pan and cook over a high heat for about 3 minutes, stirring until the prawns turn pink. Season lightly with salt and black pepper and serve immediately.

Spicy Chorizo in Olive Oil

Spanish chorizo sausage has a deliciously pungent taste.

Serves 4

INGREDIENTS
75 ml/5 tbsp extra-virgin olive oil
350 g/12 oz chorizo sausages, sliced
1 large onion, thinly sliced
roughly chopped flat leaf parsley, to garnish

1 Heat the oil in a frying pan and fry the chorizo sausage over a high heat until beginning to colour. Remove from the pan with a slotted spoon.

2 Add the onion to the pan and fry until coloured. Return the sausage slices to the pan and heat through for 1 minute.

3 Tip the mixture into a shallow serving dish and scatter with the parsley. Serve with warm bread.

e-spice Rib-stickers

Choose the meatiest spare ribs you can find, to make these a real success.

Serves 4

INGREDIENTS
1 kg/2¼ lb Chinese-style
   pork spare ribs
10 ml/2 tsp Chinese five-spice powder
2 garlic cloves, crushed
15 ml/1 tbsp grated fresh root ginger
2.5 ml/½ tsp chilli sauce
60 ml/4 tbsp soy sauce
45 ml/3 tbsp dark muscovado sugar
15 ml/1 tbsp sunflower oil
4 spring onions

1 Separate the spare ribs if still joined together (or ask your butcher to do this). Place the separated spare ribs in a large bowl.

2 Mix together the remaining ingredients, except the spring onions, and pour over the ribs. Toss to coat. Cover and leave to marinate in the fridge overnight.

3 Cook the ribs on a medium-hot barbecue, turning frequently, for 30–40 minutes. Brush occasionally with the remaining marinade.

4 Finely slice the spring onions and scatter them over the ribs, to serve.

COOK'S TIP: Make sure you buy the Chinese five-spice powder, not five-spice seasoning.

Spicy Pepper Soup

This is a highly soothing broth for winter evenings.

Serves 4–6

INGREDIENTS
30 ml/2 tbsp vegetable oil
2.5 ml/½ tsp freshly ground black pepper
5 ml/1 tsp cumin seeds
2.5 ml/½ tsp mustard seeds
1.5 ml/¼ tsp asafoetida
2 whole dried red chillies
4–6 curry leaves
2.5 ml/½ tsp turmeric
2 garlic cloves, crushed
300 ml l/½ pint/1¼ cups tomato juice
juice of 2 lemons
120 ml/4 fl oz/½ cup water
salt
chopped coriander leaves,
    to garnish

1 In a large saucepan, heat the oil and fry the pepper, cumin and mustard seeds, asafoetida, red chillies, curry leaves, turmeric and garlic until the chillies are nearly black and the garlic is golden brown.

2 Lower the heat and add the tomato juice, lemon juice, water and salt to taste. Bring the soup to the boil, then simmer gently for about 10 minutes. Pour the soup into bowls, garnish with the chopped coriander and serve.

VARIATION: If you prefer, use lime juice. Add 5 ml/1 tsp tamarind paste for extra sourness.

Chilli Pumpkin & Coconut Soup

A specially prepared spicy paste gives a kick to the rich sweetness of coconut and pumpkin in this wonderful soup.

Serves 4–6

INGREDIENTS
2 garlic cloves, crushed
4 shallots, finely chopped
2.5 ml/½ tsp shrimp paste
15 ml/1 tbsp dried shrimps, soaked for
    10 minutes and drained
1 lemon grass stalk, chopped
2 green chillies, seeded
600 ml/1 pint/2½ cups chicken stock
450 g/1 lb pumpkin, cut into 2 cm/¾ in
    thick chunks
600 ml/1 pint/2½ cups coconut cream
30 ml/2 tbsp fish sauce
5 ml/1 tsp granulated sugar
2 red chillies, seeded and finely sliced
115 g/4 oz small cooked shelled prawns
salt and freshly ground black pepper
10–12 basil leaves, to garnish

2 In a large saucepan, bring the chicken stock to the boil, add the paste and stir to dissolve.

3 Add the pumpkin and simmer for about 10–15 minutes or until the pumpkin is tender.

4 Stir in the coconut cream, then bring back to a simmer. Add the fish sauce, sugar, red chillies and freshly ground black pepper to taste.

5 Add the prawns to the soup and cook until they are heated through. Serve garnished with the basil leaves.

COOK'S TIP: Shrimp paste is made from ground shrimps fermented in brine.

1 Grind the garlic, shallots, shrimp paste, dried shrimps, lemon grass, green chillies and salt into a paste.

Hot-and-sour Prawn Soup

How hot this soup is depends upon the type of chilli used. Try tiny Thai chillies if you really want to go for the burn.

Serves 6

INGREDIENTS
225 g/8 oz raw prawns, in shells
2 lemon grass stalks
1.5 litres/2½ pints/6¼ cups vegetable stock
4 kaffir lime leaves
2 slices peeled fresh root ginger
60 ml/4 tbsp Thai fish sauce
60 ml/4 tbsp fresh lime juice
2 garlic cloves, crushed
6 spring onions, chopped
1 red chilli, seeded and
    cut into thin strips
115 g/4 oz/generous 1½ cups
    oyster mushrooms, sliced
fresh coriander leaves and kaffir lime slices,
    to garnish

1 Shell the prawns, rinse well under cold running water and set them aside. Put the shells in a large saucepan.

2 Lightly crush the lemon grass and add the stalks to the pan with the stock, lime leaves and ginger. Bring to the boil, lower the heat and simmer for 20 minutes.

3 Strain the stock into a clean pan, discarding the prawn shells and aromatics. Add the fish sauce, lime juice, garlic, spring onions, chilli and oyster mushrooms.

4 Bring to the boil, lower the heat and simmer for 5 minutes. Add the shelled prawns and cook for 2–3 minutes. Serve garnished with coriander leaves and lime slices.

COOK'S TIP: It is important that the prawns are not overcooked, or they will become tough.

Double Chilli Salsa

This is a scorchingly hot salsa for only the very brave!

Serves 4–6

INGREDIENTS
6 habanero chillies or Scotch bonnets
2 ripe tomatoes
4 standard green jalapeño chillies
30 ml/2 tbsp chopped fresh parsley
30 ml/2 tbsp olive oil
15 ml/1 tbsp balsamic or sherry vinegar
salt

1 Prepare the habanero chillies: skewer a chilli on to a metal fork and hold it in a gas flame for 2–3 minutes, turning until the skin blackens and blisters. Set aside. Use a clean dish towel to rub off the skins. Remove the tomato skins in the same way.

2 Halve the tomatoes, then use a teaspoon to scoop out and discard the seeds. Chop the flesh very finely.

3 Using a fork to hold the habanero chillies, slice them open with a sharp knife. Scrape out and discard the seeds, then finely chop the flesh.

4 Halve the jalapeño chillies, remove their seeds and finely slice them widthways into tiny strips. Combine both types of chillies, tomatoes and parsley.

5 Mix the olive oil, vinegar and salt. Pour over the salsa and cover. Chill for up to 3 days.

Salsa Verde

This green salsa is an ideal accompaniment to chargrilled squid.

Serves 4

INGREDIENTS
2–4 green chillies
8 spring onions
2 garlic cloves
50 g/2 oz salted capers
1 sprig fresh tarragon
1 bunch fresh parsley
grated rind and juice of 1 lime
juice of 1 lemon
90 ml/6 tbsp olive oil
about 15 ml/1 tbsp green Tabasco sauce
freshly ground black pepper

1 Halve and seed the chillies. Trim the onions and halve the garlic, then pulse in a food processor briefly until all the ingredients are chopped.

2 Use your fingertips to rub the excess salt off the capers but do not rinse them. Add the capers, fresh tarragon and parsley to the food processor and pulse again until they are quite finely chopped.

3 Transfer the mixture to a small bowl. Stir in the lime rind and juice, lemon juice and olive oil. Stir the mixture lightly so that the citrus juice and oil do not emulsify.

4 Add the green Tabasco sauce and pepper to taste. Chill for up to 8 hours before serving.

Chilli Bean Dip

This creamy bean dip is best served warm with triangles of grilled pitta bread or a bowl of crunchy tortilla chips.

Serves 4

INGREDIENTS
2 garlic cloves
1 onion
2 green chillies
30 ml/2 tbsp vegetable oil
5–10 ml/1–2 tsp hot chilli powder
400 g/14 oz can kidney beans
75 g/3 oz/¾ cup mature Cheddar
   cheese, grated
1 red chilli
salt and freshly ground black pepper

3 Drain the kidney beans, reserving the liquor. Blend all but 30 ml/ 2 tbsp of the beans to a smooth purée in a food processor.

1 Finely chop the garlic and onion. Halve, seed and finely chop the green chillies.

2 Heat the oil in a large sauté pan or deep frying pan and add the garlic, onion, green chillies and chilli powder. Cook gently for 5 minutes, stirring regularly to cook evenly, until the onions are softened and transparent but not browned.

4 Add the puréed beans to the pan with 30–45 ml/2–3 tbsp of the reserved liquor. Heat gently, stirring to mix well.

5 Stir in the whole beans and the Cheddar cheese. Cook gently for about 2–3 minutes, stirring until the cheese melts. Add salt and pepper to taste.

6 Seed the red chilli and cut it into tiny strips. Spoon the dip into four individual serving bowls and scatter the chilli strips over the top. Serve warm.

COOK'S TIP: For a dip with a coarser texture, do not purée the beans; instead mash them with a potato masher.

23

Fiery Citrus Salsa with Prawns

This very unusual salsa makes a fantastic marinade for any shellfish and it is also delicious drizzled over barbecued meat.

Serves 4

INGREDIENTS
1 orange
1 green apple
2 red chillies
1 garlic clove
8 fresh mint leaves
juice of 1 lemon
salt and freshly ground black pepper
large cooked prawns, to serve

1 Slice the bottom off the orange so that it will stand firmly on a chopping board. Using a sharp knife, remove the peel by slicing from the top to the bottom of the orange.

2 Holding the orange over a bowl, cut the segments away from the membrane. Squeeze any juice from the remaining membrane into the bowl.

3 Peel the apple, slice it into wedges and remove the core.

4 Halve the chillies and discard their seeds, then place them in a blender or food processor with the orange segments and juice, apple wedges, garlic and fresh mint.

5 Process until smooth. Then, with the motor running, pour in the lemon juice.

6 Season to taste with a little salt and black pepper. Pour into a bowl or small jug and serve immediately with the prawns.

VARIATION: If you're feeling really fiery, don't seed the chillies! They will make the salsa hot and fierce.

Char-grilled Tuna with Fiery Pepper Purée

Tuna is an oily fish that grills well and is meaty enough to combine successfully with quite strong flavours – even hot chilli, as in this red pepper purée, which is excellent served with fresh, crusty bread.

Serves 4

INGREDIENTS
4 tuna steaks, about 175 g/6 oz each
finely grated rind and juice of 1 lime
30 ml/2 tbsp olive oil
salt and freshly ground black pepper
lime wedges, to serve

FOR THE PEPPER PURÉE
2 red peppers, seeded and halved
1 small onion
2 garlic cloves, crushed
2 red chillies
1 slice white bread without crusts, diced
45 ml/3 tbsp olive oil, plus extra for brushing

2 To make the pepper purée, brush the pepper halves with a little olive oil and cook them, skin-side down, on a hot barbecue, until the skin is blackened.

3 Place the onion in its skin on the barbecue and cook until browned, turning it occasionally. Alternatively cook the vegetables under a hot grill – in this case the pepper halves should be skin side up.

4 Leave to cool slightly, covered with a clean cloth, and then remove the skins from the peppers and the onion.

1 Trim any skin from the tuna and place the steaks in one layer in a wide dish. Sprinkle over the lime rind and juice, oil, salt and pepper. Cover and refrigerate until required.

5 Place the peppers, onion, garlic, chillies, bread and oil in a food processor. Process until smooth. Add salt to taste. Serve with lime wedges.

6 Lift the tuna steaks from the marinade and cook them on a hot barbecue or under a hot grill for 8–10 minutes, turning once, until golden brown. Serve with the pepper purée and lime wedges.

COOK'S TIP: The pepper purée can be made in advance, by cooking the peppers and onion under a hot grill, then keep it in the fridge until you cook the fish.

27

Jamaican Spiced Cod Steaks

This fast fish dish from Kingston town is served with a spicy-hot pumpkin ragoût.

Serves 4

INGREDIENTS
finely grated rind of ½ orange
30 ml/2 tbsp black peppercorns
15 ml/1 tbsp allspice berries or
   Jamaican pepper
2.5 ml/½ tsp salt
4 cod steaks, about 175 g/6 oz each
groundnut oil, for frying
45 ml/3 tbsp chopped fresh parsley,
   to garnish
new potatoes, to serve (optional)

FOR THE PUMPKIN RAGOUT
30 ml/2 tbsp groundnut oil
1 medium onion, chopped
2.5 cm/1 in piece fresh root ginger, peeled
   and grated
450 g/1 lb pumpkin, peeled, seeded and
   chopped
3–4 shakes Tabasco sauce
30 ml/2 tbsp soft brown sugar
15 ml/1 tbsp vinegar

1 To make the ragoût, heat the oil in a heavy saucepan and add the onion and ginger. Cover and cook, stirring, for 3–4 minutes.

2 Add the chopped pumpkin, Tabasco sauce, brown sugar and vinegar, cover and cook over a low heat for 10–12 minutes, until softened.

3 Combine the orange rind, peppercorns, allspice or Jamaican pepper and salt, then crush coarsely using a pestle and mortar. (Alternatively, coarsely grind the peppercorns in a pepper mill and combine with the rind and seasoning.)

4 Scatter the spice mixture over both sides of the fish and moisten with a sprinkling of groundnut oil.

5 Heat a large frying pan and fry the cod steaks for 12 minutes, turning once to cook both sides.

6 Serve the cod steaks with a spoonful of pumpkin ragoût and new potatoes, if desired, and garnish the ragoût with chopped fresh parsley.

COOK'S TIP: This recipe can be adapted using any type of firm pink or white fish, such as haddock, whiting, monkfish, halibut or tuna.

Spiced Scallops in their Shells

Scallops are excellent steamed. When served with this spicy sauce, they make a delicious yet simple starter. Each person spoons sauce on to the scallops before eating them.

Serves 4

INGREDIENTS
8 scallops, shelled (ask the fishmonger to
    reserve the cupped side of 4 shells)
2 slices fresh root ginger, peeled
    and shredded
½ garlic clove, shredded
2 spring onions, green parts only, shredded
salt and freshly ground black pepper

FOR THE SAUCE
1 garlic clove, crushed
15 ml/1 tbsp grated fresh root ginger
2 spring onions, white parts
    only, chopped
1–2 green chillies, seeded and
    finely chopped
15 ml/1 tbsp light soy sauce
15 ml/1 tbsp dark soy sauce
10 ml/2 tsp sesame oil

2 Place 2 scallops in each shell. Season with salt and pepper, then scatter the ginger, garlic and spring onions on top. Place the shells in a bamboo steamer and steam for about 6 minutes, until the scallops look opaque (you may have to do this in batches).

3 Meanwhile, mix together all the sauce ingredients and pour into a small serving bowl.

1 Remove and discard the dark beard–like fringe and tough muscle from the scallops.

4 Carefully remove each shell from the steamer, taking care not to spill the juices, and arrange them on a serving plate with the sauce bowl in the centre. Serve at once.

Steamed Chilli Mussels

Make sure that all the mussels open when the dish is cooked as any closed ones would be dead before cooking. Add more red chillies if you really enjoy spicy food.

Serves 6

INGREDIENTS
2 red chillies
6 ripe tomatoes
30 ml/2 tbsp peanut oil
2 garlic cloves, crushed
2 shallots, finely chopped
1.2 kg/2½ lb fresh mussels
30 ml/2 tbsp white wine
30 ml/2 tbsp chopped fresh parsley,
    to garnish
French bread, to serve

3 Stir in the tomatoes and chillies and simmer for 10 minutes until slightly softened.

1 Seed the chillies and roughly chop them, washing your hands thoroughly afterwards. Roughly chop the tomatoes.

2 Heat the peanut oil in a large, heavy-based saucepan and gently sauté the garlic and shallots until soft.

4 Clean the mussels. Add the mussels and white wine to the pan, cover and cook until all the mussel shells are open: this should take about 5 minutes. Scatter the chopped parsley over the mussels. Serve in a large bowl with chunks of French bread.

Tandoori Chicken

This classic Indian dish is traditionally cooked in the tandoor, a vat-shaped clay oven heated with charcoal or wood.

Serves 4

INGREDIENTS

8 chicken pieces, such as thighs, drumsticks
    and halved breasts, skinned
60 ml/4 tbsp lemon juice
10 ml/2 tsp salt
2 garlic cloves, roughly chopped
2.5 cm/1 in piece fresh root ginger,
    peeled and roughly chopped
2 green chillies, roughly chopped
175 ml/6 fl oz/¾ cup
    natural yogurt
5 ml/1 tsp chilli powder
5 ml/1 tsp garam masala
5 ml/1 tsp ground cumin
5 ml/1 tsp ground coriander
red food colouring (optional)
30 ml/2 tbsp butter, melted
chilli powder and a sprig of fresh mint,
    to garnish
lemon wedges, salad and cucumber raita,
    to serve

1 Cut deep slashes in the chicken pieces. Mix together the lemon juice and 5ml/1tsp salt and rub over the chicken. Cover and leave to marinate for 10 minutes for the flavours to blend well.

2 Put the garlic, ginger and chillies into a food processor or blender and process until smooth.

3 Add the mixture to the yogurt, remaining salt, chilli powder, garam masala, ground cumin and ground coriander and mix well.

4 Brush the chicken pieces with food colouring, if using, and put into a dish. Add the marinade and chill overnight. Preheat the oven to 220°C/425°F/Gas 7.

5 Put the chicken in a roasting tin and bake for 40 minutes, basting with butter. Garnish with chilli powder and mint and serve with lemon wedges, salad and cucumber raita.

COOK'S TIP: The traditional bright red colour associated with this dish is derived from food colouring. This is only optional and may be omitted if you wish.

Chicken Vindaloo

This is considered rather a hot curry and is probably one of the best-known Indian dishes, especially in the West.

Serves 4

INGREDIENTS
1 large potato
150 ml/¼ pint/⅔ cup malt vinegar
7.5 ml/1½ tsp crushed
    coriander seeds
5 ml/1 tsp crushed cumin seeds
7.5 ml/1½ tsp chilli powder
1.5 ml/¼ tsp ground turmeric
5 ml/1 tsp crushed garlic
5 ml/1 tsp crushed fresh root ginger
5 ml/1 tsp salt
7.5 ml/1½ tsp paprika
15 ml/1 tbsp tomato purée
large pinch of ground fenugreek
300 ml/½ pint/1¼ cups water
225 g/8 oz boned skinless chicken breasts,
    cubed
15 ml/1 tbsp corn oil
2 medium onions, sliced
4 curry leaves
2 green chillies, chopped

1 Peel the potato, cut it into large, irregular shapes, place in a bowl of water and set aside.

2 Mix the vinegar with the coriander, cumin, chilli powder, turmeric, garlic, ginger, salt, paprika, tomato purée, fenugreek and water. Stir well until blended. Pour this mixture over the chicken and set aside.

3 Heat the oil in a non-stick wok or frying pan and fry the onions with the curry leaves for 3–4 minutes.

4 Lower the heat and add the chicken mixture to the wok or frying pan. Continue to stir for a further 2 minutes.

5 Drain the potato pieces and add to the pan. Cover with a lid and cook over a medium to low heat for 10 minutes or until the sauce has thickened slightly and the chicken and potato pieces are cooked through.

6 Add the chopped green chillies before serving.

COOK'S TIP: The best thing to drink with a hot curry is either iced water or a yogurt-based lassi.

Chilli Chicken

This fiery, hot curry is not for the faint-hearted.

Serves 4

INGREDIENTS
30 ml/2 tbsp tomato purée
2 garlic cloves, roughly chopped
2 green chillies, roughly chopped
5 dried red chillies
2.5 ml/½ tsp salt
1.5 ml/¼ tsp sugar
5 ml/1 tsp chilli powder
2.5 ml/½ tsp paprika
15 ml/1 tbsp curry paste
30 ml/2 tbsp oil
2.5 ml/½ tsp cumin seeds
1 onion, finely chopped
2 bay leaves
5 ml/1 tsp ground coriander
5 ml/1 tsp ground cumin
1.5 ml/¼ tsp ground turmeric
400 g/14 oz can chopped tomatoes
150 ml/¼ pint/⅔ cup water
8 chicken thighs, skinned
5 ml/1 tsp garam masala
sliced green chillies, to garnish
chapatis and natural yogurt, to serve

1 Put the tomato purée, garlic, green and dried red chillies, salt, sugar, chilli powder, paprika and curry paste into a food processor or blender and process to a smooth paste.

2 Heat the oil in a large saucepan and fry the cumin seeds for 2 minutes. Add the onion and bay leaves and fry for about 5 minutes.

3 Add the chilli paste and fry for 2–3 minutes. Add the remaining ground spices and cook for 2 minutes. Add the chopped tomatoes and water. Bring to the boil and simmer for 5 minutes, until the sauce thickens.

4 Add the chicken and garam masala. Cover and simmer for 25–30 minutes, until the chicken is tender. Serve with chapatis and natural yogurt, garnished with sliced green chillies.

k Chops with Spicy Lemon & Garlic Sauce

Tabasco gives a fiery flavour to this recipe.

Serves 4

INGREDIENTS
4 pork chops
115 g/4 oz/½ cup butter
½ lemon
15 ml/1 tbsp Worcestershire sauce
7.5 ml/1½ tsp Tabasco sauce
1 garlic clove, finely chopped
salt and freshly ground black pepper
grilled sweet peppers and tomatoes, to serve

1 Preheat the grill. Arrange the chops in the grill pan, but do not place them under the grill. Melt the butter in a small, non-aluminium saucepan. Squeeze in the juice of the lemon and bring to simmering point.

2 Add the Worcestershire and Tabasco sauces and the garlic and continue cooking gently, without browning the garlic, for about 5 minutes. Season with salt and pepper.

3 Brush the tops of the chops liberally with the sauce, place the pan under the grill and cook for about 5 minutes, until they begin to brown.

4 Turn the chops and brush with more sauce. Grill for a further 5 minutes or so, depending on the thickness of the chops: ensure that they are cooked through. You can trickle a little more of the sauce over to serve. Accompany the chops with grilled sweet peppers and tomatoes.

COOK'S TIP: This makes a very good sauce for barbecue cooking as well as for indoor grilling. On the barbecue it complements most vegetables and can be an accompaniment to meat and fish. Under the grill it is also good with chicken or duck breasts or with lamb steaks.

Hot Pepperoni Pizza

There is nothing more mouth-watering than a freshly baked pizza, especially when the topping includes pepperoni and red chillies.

Serves 4

INGREDIENTS
225 g/8 oz/2 cups strong white bread flour
10 ml/2 tsp easy-blend dried yeast
5 ml/1 tsp sugar
2.5 ml/½ tsp salt
15 ml/1 tbsp olive oil
175 ml/6 fl oz/¾ cup mixed hand-hot milk
    and water

FOR THE TOPPING
400 g/14 oz can chopped tomatoes, drained
    or 450 g/1 lb fresh tomatoes, skinned
    and chopped
2 garlic cloves, crushed
5 ml/1 tsp dried oregano
225 g/8 oz/2 cups Mozzarella cheese,
    coarsely grated
2 dried red chillies, crumbled
225 g/8 oz pepperoni, sliced
30 ml/2 tbsp drained capers
fresh oregano, to garnish

1 Sift the flour into a bowl. Stir in the yeast, sugar and salt. Make a well in the centre. Stir the olive oil into the milk and water, then stir the mixture into the flour. Mix to a soft dough.

2 Knead the dough, pulling the outer edge to the centre, on a lightly floured surface for 5–10 minutes, until it is smooth and elastic.

3 Return it to the clean, lightly oiled bowl and cover with clear film. Leave in a warm place for about 30 minutes.

4 Preheat the oven to 220°C/425°F/ Gas 7. Turn the dough out on to a floured surface and knead for 1 minute. Halve it and roll each piece out to a 25 cm/10 in circle. Place on two lightly oiled pizza trays.

5 To make the topping, mix the tomatoes, garlic and oregano. Spread half the mixture over each dough round, leaving a margin around the edge. Use a quarter of the Mozzarella on each pizza. Bake for 7–10 minutes, until golden.

6 Sprinkle the crumbled chillies, the pepperoni and capers over the pizzas. Add the remaining Mozzarella. Return to the oven and bake for 7–10 minutes. Garnish with oregano.

Jambalaya

This Cajun dish comes from the deep south of the USA. It contains a wonderful combination of rice, meat and fish, with a kick of chilli.

Serves 6

INGREDIENTS

450 g/1 lb boneless, skinless chicken thighs
225 g/8 oz chorizo or spicy sausages
5 celery sticks
1 red pepper, seeded
1 green pepper, seeded
about 30 ml/2 tbsp oil
225 g/8 oz onions, roughly chopped
2 garlic cloves, crushed
10 ml/2 tsp mild chilli powder
2.5 ml/½ tsp ground ginger
300 g/11 oz/generous 1½ cups long-grain white rice
900 ml/1½ pints/3¾ cups chicken stock
175 g/6 oz cooked shelled prawns
salt and freshly ground black pepper
12 cooked prawns in shells, with heads removed, to garnish

1 Cut the chicken and chorizo into small, bite-size pieces. Cut the celery and peppers into thin 5 cm/2 in julienne strips.

2 Heat the oil in a very large frying pan or large saucepan and cook the chicken until golden. Remove with a slotted spoon and drain on kitchen paper. Cook the chorizo for 2 minutes and drain on kitchen paper.

3 Add the celery and peppers and cook for 3–4 minutes. Drain on kitchen paper. Cook the onions and garlic for 3 minutes. Add the chilli powder and ground ginger and cook for 1 minute.

4 Stir in the rice, cook for 1 minute. Add the stock, replace the chicken and bring to the boil. Cover and simmer for 12–15 minutes, stirring occasionally, until the rice is tender and the liquid absorbed. Add more water, if necessary, during cooking. Gently add the chorizo, peppers, celery and peeled prawns and stir until hot. Season and garnish with the 12 prawns

Rice Noodles with Beef & Spicy Black Bean Sauce

This is an excellent combination – beef and peppers with a chilli sauce tossed with silky smooth rice noodles.

Serves 4

INGREDIENTS
450 g/1 lb fresh rice noodles
60 ml/4 tbsp vegetable oil
1 onion, finely sliced
2 garlic cloves, finely chopped
2 slices peeled fresh root ginger,
    finely chopped
225 g/8 oz mixed peppers, seeded and
    cut into strips
350 g/12 oz rump steak, finely sliced
    against the grain
45 ml/3 tbsp fermented black beans,
    rinsed in warm water, drained
    and chopped
30 ml/2 tbsp soy sauce
30 ml/2 tbsp oyster sauce
15 ml/1 tbsp chilli black bean sauce
15 ml/1 tbsp cornflour
120 ml/4 fl oz/½ cup stock or water
2 spring onions, finely chopped, and
    2 red chillies, seeded and finely sliced,
    to garnish

1 Rinse the noodles under hot water; drain well. Heat half the oil in a wok or large frying pan, swirling it around. Add the onion, garlic, ginger and mixed pepper strips. Stir-fry for 3–5 minutes, then remove with a slotted spoon and keep hot.

2 Add the remaining oil to the wok. When it is hot, add the sliced steak and fermented black beans and stir-fry over a high heat for 5 minutes or until the meat is cooked.

3 In a small bowl, blend the soy sauce, oyster sauce and chilli black bean sauce with the cornflour and stock or water until smooth. Add the mixture to the wok, then return the onion mixture to the wok and cook, stirring, for 1 minute.

4 Add the noodles and mix lightly. Stir over a medium heat until the noodles are heated through. Add seasoning if necessary. Serve at once, garnished with the chopped spring onions and chillies.

Mexican Enchiladas

Spicy chorizo sausage makes a filling-with-a-kick for this colourful version of a classic Mexican dish.

Serves 6

INGREDIENTS
4 dried ancho chillies
450 g/1 lb tomatoes, peeled, seeded and
    chopped
1 onion, finely chopped
1 garlic clove, finely chopped
15 ml/1 tbsp chopped fresh coriander
lard or corn oil, for frying
250 ml/8 fl oz/1 cup soured cream
4 chorizo sausages, skinned and chopped
18 freshly prepared unbaked corn tortillas
50 g/2 oz/⅔ cup grated Parmesan cheese
salt and freshly ground black pepper

1 Roast the ancho chillies in a dry frying pan over moderate heat for 1–2 minutes, shaking the pan frequently. When they have cooled, carefully slit the chillies, discard the stems and seeds and tear the pods into pieces. Put in a bowl, add warm water to just cover and soak for 20 minutes.

2 Tip the chillies, with a little of the soaking water, into a food processor. Add the tomatoes, onion, garlic and coriander and process to a purée.

3 Heat 15 ml/1 tbsp lard or oil in a saucepan. Add the purée and cook gently over a moderate heat, stirring, for 3–4 minutes. Season to taste with salt and pepper and then stir in the soured cream. Remove the pan from the heat and set it aside.

4 Heat a further 15 ml/1 tbsp lard or oil in a small frying pan and sauté the chorizo for a few minutes until lightly browned. Moisten with a little of the sauce and set the pan aside.

5 Preheat the oven to 180°C/350°F/ Gas 4. Heat 30 ml/2 tbsp lard or oil in a frying pan. Dip a tortilla in the sauce and add to the pan. Cook for a few seconds, shaking the pan gently, turn over and briefly fry the other side.

6 Slide the tortilla on to a plate, top with some of the sausage mixture and roll up. Pack the prepared tortillas in a single layer in a baking dish. Pour the sauce over, sprinkle with Parmesan and bake for about 20 minutes or until bubbling hot.

COOK'S TIP: The method of dipping the tortillas first in sauce, then quickly cooking them, gives the best flavour. If you prefer, fry the plain tortillas very quickly, then dip them in the sauce, stuff and roll.

hilli con Carne

Two chillies add plenty of fire to this Tex-Mex classic.

Serves 6

INGREDIENTS
225 g/8 oz/1¼ cups dried black beans
500 g/1¼ lb braising steak
30 ml/2 tbsp oil
2 onions, chopped
1 garlic clove, crushed
1 green chilli, seeded and finely chopped
15 ml/1 tbsp paprika
10 ml/2 tsp ground cumin
10 ml/2 tsp ground coriander
400 g/14 oz can chopped tomatoes
300 ml/½ pint/1¼ cups beef stock
1 dried red chilli, crumbled
5 ml/1 tsp hot pepper sauce
1 red pepper, seeded and chopped
30 ml/2 tbsp fresh coriander leaves
salt
plain boiled rice, to serve

1 Put the beans in a saucepan. Add water to cover, bring to the boil and boil vigorously for 10–15 minutes. Drain, tip into a clean bowl, cover with cold water and leave to soak for about 8 hours or overnight.

2 Preheat the oven to 150°C/300°F/ Gas 2. Cut the beef into very small dice. Heat the oil in a large flameproof casserole. Add the onions, garlic and green chilli and cook them gently for 5 minutes, until soft. Using a slotted spoon, transfer the mixture to a plate.

3 Increase the heat and brown the meat, then stir in the paprika, cumin and ground coriander.

4 Add the tomatoes, stock, dried chilli and hot pepper sauce. Drain the beans and add them to the casserole, with enough water to cover. Bring to simmering point, cover and cook in the oven for 2 hours. Stir occasionally, adding extra water if necessary.

5 Season with salt and add the red pepper. Return to the oven and cook for 30 minutes more, until the meat and beans are tender. Scatter the fresh coriander over the chilli and serve with the boiled rice.

Spicy Kebabs with Tomato & Olive Salsa

The mix of aromatic spices, garlic and lemon gives these kebabs a wonderful flavour; a fiery salsa makes the perfect accompaniment.

Serves 4

INGREDIENTS
2 garlic cloves, crushed
60 ml/4 tbsp lemon juice
30 ml/2 tbsp olive oil
1 dried red chilli, crushed
5 ml/1 tsp ground cumin
5 ml/1 tsp ground coriander
500 g/1¼ lb lean lamb,
    cut into 4 cm/1½ in cubes
8 bay leaves
salt and freshly ground black pepper

FOR THE TOMATO AND OLIVE SALSA
175 g/6 oz/1½ cups mixed pitted green
    and black olives, roughly chopped
1 small red onion, finely chopped
4 plum tomatoes, peeled and finely
    chopped
1 red chilli, seeded and finely
    chopped
30 ml/2 tbsp olive oil

1 Mix the garlic, lemon juice, olive oil, chilli, cumin and coriander in a large, shallow dish. Add the lamb cubes, with salt and pepper to taste. Mix well. Cover and marinate in a cool place for 2 hours to ensure that the flavours are well absorbed by the cubes of lamb.

2 Make the salsa. Put the olives, onion, tomatoes, chilli and olive oil in a bowl. Stir in salt and pepper to taste. Mix well, cover and set aside.

3 Remove the lamb from the marinade and divide the cubes among four skewers, adding the bay leaves at intervals. Grill over a barbecue, on a ridged iron grill pan or under a hot grill, turning occasionally, for 10 minutes, until the lamb is browned and crisp on the outside and pink and juicy inside. Serve with the salsa.

ced Lamb with Chillies

Lean pieces of lamb are marinated in yogurt laced with a combination of aromatic spices before they are cooked.

Serves 4

INGREDIENTS
225 g/8 oz lean lamb fillet
120 ml/4 fl oz/½ cup natural yogurt
1.5 ml/¼ tsp ground cardamom
5 ml/1 tsp peeled and crushed fresh
  root ginger
5 ml/1 tsp crushed garlic
5 ml/1 tsp chilli powder
5 ml/1 tsp garam masala
5 ml/1 tsp salt
15 ml/1 tbsp corn oil
2 medium onions, chopped
1 bay leaf
300 ml/½ pint/1¼ cups water
2 red chillies, seeded and
  sliced lengthways
2 green chillies, seeded and
  sliced lengthways
30 ml/2 tbsp fresh coriander leaves

2 Mix together the yogurt, cardamom, crushed ginger and garlic, chilli powder, garam masala and salt. Add the lamb and leave for about 1 hour to marinate.

3 Heat the oil in a non-stick wok or frying pan and fry the onions for 3–5 minutes until they are soft and golden brown.

4 Add the bay leaf, then add the lamb with the yogurt and spices and stir-fry for 2–3 minutes over a medium heat.

5 Pour over the water, cover and cook for 15–20 minutes over a low heat, checking occasionally. Once the water has evaporated, stir-fry the mixture for 1 further minute.

1 Using a sharp knife, cut the lamb into even-size strips.

6 Add the red and green chillies and the fresh coriander and serve.

Pasta with Tomato & Chilli Sauce

This is a speciality of the Lazio region of Italy – its Italian name *Pasta Arrabbiata* means rabid or angry, and describes the heat that comes from the chilli. This quick version is made with bottled sugocasa.

Serves 4

INGREDIENTS
500 g/1¼ lb sugocasa (see Cook's Tip)
2 garlic cloves, crushed
150 ml/¼ pint/⅔ cup dry white wine
15 ml/1 tbsp sun-dried tomato purée
1 red chilli
300 g/11 oz penne or tortiglioni
60 ml/4 tbsp finely chopped fresh
    flat leaf parsley
salt and freshly ground black pepper
grated Pecorino cheese, to serve

2 Remove the chilli from the sauce and add half the parsley. Taste for seasoning. If you prefer a hotter taste, chop some or all of the chilli and return it to the sauce.

1 Put the sugocasa, garlic, wine, tomato purée and whole chilli in a saucepan and bring to the boil. Cover and simmer gently. Drop the pasta into a large saucepan of rapidly boiling salted water and simmer for 10–12 minutes or until *al dente*.

3 Drain the pasta and tip into a warmed large bowl. Pour the sauce over the pasta and toss to mix. Serve at once, sprinkled with grated Pecorino and the remaining parsley.

COOK'S TIP: Sugocasa is a coarser version of passata.

Vegetable Couscous with Saffron & Harissa

A North African favourite, this spicy dish makes an excellent meal for vegetarians.

Serves 4

INGREDIENTS
45 ml/3 tbsp olive oil
1 onion, chopped
2 garlic cloves, crushed
5 ml/1 tsp each ground
   cumin and paprika
400 g/14 oz can chopped tomatoes
300 ml/½ pint/1¼ cups vegetable stock
1 cinnamon stick
generous pinch of saffron strands
4 baby aubergines, quartered
8 baby courgettes, trimmed
8 baby carrots
225 g/8 oz/1⅓ cups couscous
425 g/15 oz can chick-peas, drained
175 g/6 oz/¾ cup prunes
45 ml/3 tbsp chopped fresh parsley
45 ml/3 tbsp chopped fresh coriander
10–15 ml/2–3 tsp harissa
salt

1 Heat the olive oil in a large saucepan. Add the onion and garlic and cook gently for 5 minutes, until soft. Add the cumin and paprika and cook, stirring, for 1 minute.

2 Add the tomatoes, stock, cinnamon stick, saffron, vegetables and salt. Bring to the boil, cover, lower the heat and cook for 20 minutes.

3 Line a steamer, metal sieve or colander with a double thickness of muslin. Soak the couscous according to the instructions on the packet. Add the chick-peas and prunes to the vegetables and cook for 5 minutes.

4 Fork the couscous to break up any lumps and spread it in the prepared steamer. Place on top of the vegetables, cover, and cook for 5 minutes until the couscous is hot.

5 Stir the parsley and coriander into the vegetables. Heap the couscous on to a warmed serving plate. Using a slotted spoon, arrange the vegetables on top. Spoon over a little sauce and toss gently to combine. Stir the harissa into the remaining sauce and serve in a separate bowl.

Okra with Green Mango & Lentils

If you like okra, you'll love this spicy and tangy dish.

Serves 4

INGREDIENTS

115 g/4 oz/½ cup yellow lentils (toor dhal)
45ml/3 tbsp corn oil
2.5 ml/½ tsp onion seeds
2 medium onions, sliced
25 ml/½ tsp ground fenugreek
5 ml/1 tsp crushed fresh root ginger
5 ml/1 tsp crushed garlic
7.5 ml/1½ tsp chilli powder
1.5 ml/¼ tsp ground turmeric
5 ml/1 tsp ground coriander
1 green (unripe) mango, peeled and sliced
450 g/1 lb okra, cut into 1 cm/½ in pieces
7.5 ml/1½ tsp salt
2 red chillies, seeded and sliced
30 ml/2 tbsp chopped fresh coriander
1 tomato, sliced

1 Wash the lentils thoroughly and put in a saucepan with enough water to cover. Bring to the boil and cook until soft but not mushy. Drain and set to one side.

2 Heat the oil in a deep round-bottomed frying pan or a wok and fry the onion seeds until they begin to pop. Add the onions and fry until golden brown. Lower the heat and add the ground fenugreek, ginger, garlic, chilli powder, turmeric and ground coriander. Stir well to mix.

3 Throw in the mango slices and the okra. Stir well and add the salt, red chillies and fresh coriander. Stir-fry for about 3 minutes or until the okra is just cooked.

4 Finally, add the cooked lentils and sliced tomato and cook for a further 3 minutes. Serve hot.

COOK'S TIP: This recipe is delicious served alone or with basmati rice.

Deep-fried Courgettes with Chilli Sauce

Crunchy-coated courgettes are great served with a fiery tomato sauce.

Serves 2

INGREDIENTS
15 ml/1 tbsp olive oil
1 onion, finely chopped
1 red chilli, seeded and finely diced
10 ml/2 tsp hot chilli powder
400 g/14 oz can chopped tomatoes
1 vegetable stock cube
50 ml/2 fl oz/¼ cup hot water
450 g/1 lb courgettes
150 ml/¼ pint/⅔ cup milk
50 g/2 oz/½ cup plain flour
oil, for deep-frying
salt and freshly ground black pepper
thyme sprigs, to garnish

TO SERVE
lettuce leaves
watercress sprigs
slices of seeded bread

1 Heat the oil in a pan. Add the onion and cook for 2–3 minutes. Add the chilli. Stir in the chilli powder and cook for 30 seconds.

2 Add the tomatoes. Crumble in the stock cube and stir in the water. Cover and cook for 10 minutes.

3 Meanwhile, top and tail the courgettes. Cut into 5 mm/¼ in slices.

4 Pour the milk into one shallow dish and spread out the flour in another. Dip the sliced courgettes first in the milk, then into the flour, until evenly coated.

5 Heat the oil for deep frying to 180°C/350°F or until a cube of bread, when added to the oil, browns in 30–45 seconds. Add the sliced courgettes in batches and deep fry for 3–4 minutes, until golden and crisp. Drain on kitchen paper.

6 Place 2 or 3 lettuce leaves on each serving plate. Add a few sprigs of watercress and fan out the bread slices to one side. Season the sauce, spoon some on to each plate, top with the crisp courgettes and garnish with the thyme sprigs. Serve at once.

Index

This edition published by Hermes House

Hermes House is an imprint of
Anness Publishing Limited
Hermes House, 88–89 Blackfriars Road, London SE1 8HA

Publisher: Joanna Lorenz
Editor: Valerie Ferguson
Series Designer: Bobbie Colgate Stone
Designer: Andrew Heath
Editorial Reader: Felicity Forster
Production Controller: Joanna King

Recipes contributed by: Angela Boggiano, Kit Chan,
Nicola Diggins, Matthew Drennan, Sarah Edmonds,
Joanna Farrow, Rafi Fernandez, Christine France, Silvano
Franco, Shirley Gill, Shehzad Husain, Manisha Kanani,
Elisabeth Lambert Ortiz, Ruby Le Bois, Lesley Mackley,
Sue Maggs, Steven Wheeler, Liz Trigg, Jeni Wright.

Photography: William Adams-Lingwood, Karl Adamson,
Edward Allwright, David Armstrong , Steve Baxter,
James Duncan, Michelle Garrett, Amanda Heywood,
Ferguson Hill, Janine Hosegood, David Jordan, Don Last,
Patrick McLeavy, Thomas Odulate.

© Anness Publishing Limited 1999, updated 2000
2 3 4 5 6 7 8 9 10

Notes

For all recipes, quantities are given in both metric and
imperial measures and, where appropriate, measures
are also given in standard cups and spoons.
Follow one set, but not a mixture, because they are
not interchangeable.

Standard spoon and cup measures are level.

1 tsp = 5 ml
1 tbsp = 15 ml
1 cup = 250 ml/8 fl oz

Australian standard tablespoons are 20 ml.
Australian readers should use 3 tsp in place of 1 tbsp
for measuring small quantities of gelatine, cornflour,
salt, etc.

Medium eggs are used
unless otherwise stated.

Printed and bound in China